The Essentia

T

S-SE...

S1, S2, S3/S3C, S4C & V8S 1986 to 1994

Your marque expert:
Richard Kitchen

VELOCE PUBLISHING
THE PUBLISHER OF FINE AUTOMOTIVE BOOKS

www.veloce.co.uk

First published in October 2018 by Veloce Publishing Limited, Veloce House, Parkway Farm Business Park, Middle Farm Way, Poundbury, Dorchester DT1 3AR, England. Tel +44 (0)1305 260068 / Fax 01305 250479 / e-mail info@veloce.co.uk / web www.veloce.co.uk or www.velocebooks.com.
ISBN: 978-1-787112-90-2 UPC: 6-36847-01290-8.
British Library Cataloguing in Publication Data – A catalogue record for this book is available from the British Library. Typesetting, design and page make-up all by Veloce Publishing Ltd on Apple Mac. Printed in India by Replika Press.

Introduction
– the purpose of this book

1981 was one of the biggest years in TVR's history. That was the year Peter Wheeler took the helm, and soon realised what it desperately needed was a pretty sports car to replace the wedge-shaped Tasmin, which was proving too costly to produce for the entry-level sports car market.

Five years later, the car Wheeler had come up with was ready. Baring slightly more than a passing resemblance to the M-Series-based 3000S model of 1978, the S-Series was, in fact, an all-new car. The fact that it so closely resembled its forebear was intentional. After all, why change a proven formula?

The brief for the new car was simple: It needed to be efficient to build, and to use as few parts as possible, from as few sources as possible. By shaving the factory build time from a reported 400 hours for the Tasmin to just 250 hours for the S, TVR more than managed to achieve

Andy Hills' beautiful V8S.
(www.myfavouritephotos.com)

that brief, and total factory production for 1987 doubled over the previous year. To say it's the car that saved TVR in the 1980s is no overstatement, and revered models such as the Griffith and Chimaera that followed owe their existence to the little S.

Though the first few models were built in 1986, production didn't enter full-swing until 1987, by which time the S model had phased out the entry-level Tasmin completely.

The model initially featured Ford's fuel-injected 160bhp 2.8 'Cologne' V6 engine (as found in the Capri 2.8i), cloaked in a classic-esque fibreglass body tub atop an all-new tubular steel chassis. Suspension was via double wishbones at the front, with a semi-trailing arm arrangement at the rear (deliberately similar to the Ford Sierra's setup). Brakes, transmission, differential and suspension uprights were also borrowed from Ford's mainstream runabout.

Left to right: V8S; S3; S2; S1. (www.myfavouritephotos.com)

Ford phased out the 2.8 unit in favour of the improved 2.9 a couple of years later. As a direct result, TVR introduced the S2 model, featuring the aforementioned 2.9 engine, which now controlled its fuel-injection electronically. The increase in claimed power output was slight, but the torque output was noticeably improved over the 2.8 and was accessible lower in the rev range. TVR continued to produce the S-Series with this engine until 1994, when the last S4C ('C' denoted the addition of catalytic converters) was produced. The halo model is the V8S; an S-Series fitted with a 3947cc Rover V8 engine, limited-slip differential, disc brakes all-round, widened suspension track and a strengthened chassis to deal with the extra torque. These were produced in limited numbers alongside the V6 models between 1991 and 1994.

Approximately 2600 S-Series cars were produced in total, and today many still reside in driveways all over the world, from Nottingham to New Zealand!

The author's 1989 S1 – one of the very last 2.8s produced.

Thanks

Brian Hosfield and Trevor Cooper (and Surface & Design for Trevor's time!); Alex Robbins; Andy Hills; Paul Hewitt (cover car), Richard Jarvis, Mike Phillips (and the S-ownership online community); Andrew Burniston; and lastly my long-suffering wife Natalie and sons Jack, Liam & Ryan for their patience and support!

Contents

The Essential Buyer's Guide™ currency
At the time of publication a BG unit of currency " ● " equals approximately £1.00/US$1.34/Euro 1.14. Please adjust to suit current exchange rates using Sterling as the base currency.

1 Is it the right car for you?
– marriage guidance

Tall & short drivers

The longer-legged driver might consider a later car (S3/S4/V8S), as the length of the doors was extended by 110mm, which noticeably aids entry and egress. Once inside, it's generally an easy, comfortable driving position in all variants; Peter Wheeler was 6ft 6in tall, and he only built cars he could fit in!

Earlier, smaller doors of a red S2 versus later, larger doors of a blue S3.
(www.myfavouritephotos.com)

Controls

The biggest difference here is the contrasting dashboard layouts of the early and later cars. The later dashboard design coincided with the enlarged door openings, so if you want the earlier dashboard, you can't have the larger doors. The gearshift is located quite far back in the centre console, but the steering column controls are straightforward to operate, and the brakes are servo-assisted. It should be noted that no TVR S-Series were offered with an automatic transmission or power steering.

S1 and S2 models (left) featured a distinctive 'wrap-around' dash, while later models S3/S4/V8S (right) had a traditional upright affair, often featuring wood veneer.
(www.myfavouritephotos.com)

Will it fit in the garage?

The S-Series is a relatively compact car. At under 4 metres long (158in) and 1.67 metres wide (66in), the S will comfortably fit inside most single garages.

Parts availability & costs

Parts availability isn't a big problem for the S-Series. It's a car built 'by hand,' so anything somebody once made before, somebody else could make again. Many of the mechanicals are straight from the classic Ford parts catalogues, and while there are a few hard-to-find items, some parts suppliers have taken to having certain components reproduced.

Insurance

Most insurance companies recognise the S-Series as a classic, and offer limited-use policies that could undercut the premium of a family saloon. Some companies require that a Category 1 or 2 immobiliser is fitted though, so check the smallprint.

Investment potential

The residuals for this specialist British sports car have been exceptionally low for a number of years now. The market 'bottomed out' between 2005 and 2010, and values have slowly been climbing since, with the V8S owners likely to see the best returns.

Quirks

TVR made quirky cars; the S is no different. Most will feature a speedometer and tachometer that sweep downwards from rest, rather than up, and these gauges (along with all the others) will likely steam up while driving. This is completely

Your single garage should be large enough to accommodate an S. (P Bastiaansen)

The original front indicators (taken from a Sherpa van) are notoriously difficult to source. (M Roberts)

The market value of the S can only take off! Sadly, the Vulcan is forever grounded. (D Murch)

normal, as is the impression of 'scuttle-shake,' a trait most commonly noticed on the early models due to lateral movement within the body tub. Add to this windows that don't fully drop down, a bonnet that seemingly doesn't fully open up, and, on the V6 models, a battery charge lamp that doesn't extinguish from start-up until you rev the engine.

Advantages

They're surprisingly practical cars, mechanically tough and fantastic fun. They're brimming with character, and the running costs are fairer than you'd think. They all sound fantastic too. When you're sans roof on the open road, you won't believe how little you paid to be there!

Steamy dials – completely normal.

Disadvantages

It's a hand-built car, so expect rattles and leaks (though build did improve with the later models). While it's often easy to find one for sale, it's not as easy to find a *good* one. All S-Series require frequent fettling, and will deteriorate quickly without routine maintenance.

Alternatives

The S-Series is a difficult car to place in the market, partly because they're currently so undervalued, and partly because their values vary within the model lineup so much. If the soft top roof is a must, then you have newer rivals like the Mazda MX-5, MGF or Lotus Elan M100, which could be had for the cost of a fair S1/S2. If classics are what you desire, the Triumph TR7/8, Jensen Healey or MGB might be in a similar budget. The values of some of the S4 and V8S models put them in competition with Porsches of the era, and even other TVRs, such as the later Chimaera.

The author's S1 being enjoyed by *Autocar*'s Alex Robbins. (John Bradshaw/*Autocar*)

2 Cost considerations
– affordable, or a money pit?

Though you should examine any potential TVR S purchase in close detail, there are three main areas to concern yourself with. In order of importance, these are:

The chassis
The most important thing to check out, because this will undoubtedly be the most costly thing to refurbish. Quick outrigger replacements tend to start at around ●x1500, but if you want to have the chassis restored properly, you could easily spend ●x7000 at a specialist, or more should you have additional mechanical work carried out at the same time.

You could easily spend more than the value of an S-Series putting right a rusted chassis. (Southways Automotive Ltd)

The bodywork
GRP can be difficult to work with, and it takes a specialist bodyshop to get good results. Specialist bodyshops charge specialist bodyshop prices, so check the bodywork for damage, cracking and crazing. A high-quality full-body respray can often cost ●x4000 or more on a car such as this, especially if the current paintwork is exceptionally bad, or full of microblisters.

You won't find dents on an S, just cracks! Some are more obvious than others ... (Southways Automotive Ltd)

The interior
A full interior retrim at a professional trimmer can be around ●x3000, so make sure the interior is either in good order, or the car is priced to reflect it.

Tatty seats might be one thing, but throw in a small tear in the hood, and some UV-damaged carpets, and the cost of repair or replacement could accelerate quicker than the car itself. (Southways Automotive Ltd)

3 Living with an S-Series
– will you get along together?

TVR S-Series are lightweight, front-engined/rear-wheel drive sports cars. They're best suited to faster rural roads, yet are agile enough to be enjoyed on tighter lanes, too. They're also great touring companions, and have a reasonably capacious boot.

There isn't much in the motoring world that can rival a TVR for roof-off motoring on a summer's day. (G Sharpe/I Renwick)

All S-Series are convertibles, and feature the same two-piece folding roof setup that TVR used across all of its convertible models from the Tasmin onwards. A fold-down hoop behind the driver is fixed in place by two struts in front of the flexible rear screen which lock in an 'over-centre' fashion. Positioned between this and the windscreen surround are two targa panels (the S is the only TVR to feature split targa panels), which can be either left in place, sandwiched in tension between the rear hoop and the windscreen surround, or removed and stowed in the boot.

Full roof, half roof (with just the targa panels removed), full-convertible (targa panels removed, and rear roof hoop folded down). The choice is yours!

As the doors are pillarless, the driver can enjoy the full open-top experience, with accompanying soundtrack! Also, when the roof is on you still have a rigid panel above your head, unlike most soft tops. The only drawback is that it can be quite fiddly to remove or refit the roof, especially when compared with the one-piece fold-down systems fitted to similar cars.

Whichever engine your S is propelled by, they all rumble into life and tingle with excitement as they settle into a purposeful idle.

Targa roof panels stowed in their original factory bags in the boot, next to the space-saver spare wheel.

One of the best aspects of the S is the sense of occasion when you drop down into its low-slung seat and flip the key. Be aware that these are, generally speaking, loud cars. If you prefer your exhaust on the quieter side, the catalyst-equipped cars won't annoy the neighbours (quite) as much.

On the move, the S-Series is a very rewarding drive. With its engine positioned behind the front axle-line, it's a well-balanced machine that flows seamlessly from corner to corner. The steering – while fairly heavy at manoeuvring speeds – lightens up once on the move, and is geared to perfectly suit the nature of the car. The ride can be choppy when the going gets rough, but across undulating surfaces and less-than-perfect tarmac, the S is a composed yet responsive companion. You do have to be cautious with speed humps and similar obstacles in the road as the exhaust hangs very low underneath the car, and willingly connects with the road at any opportunity. There's also nowhere to rest your left foot when on the move. Visibility is reasonably good, though the Citroën CX door mirrors fitted to later models noticeably improve things looking rearward.

The 'bunny ear' door mirrors (top) of the earlier red car restrict rear visibility compared with the Citroën-sourced units (bottom) of later models.
(www.myfavouritephotos.com)

Cars of a more quirky nature carry quirky traits. There are a number of ways a TVR S-Series will do its level best to keep you on your toes. Even rudimentary tasks such as filling it up with fuel can prove tricky to the uninitiated, as the majority of forecourt pump nozzles will need to be held in an awkward position to prevent overspill, or premature 'clicking' from the pump. And opening the bonnet? Well, make sure the nose of the car is nowhere near a kerb!

In its day, the S was seen as a high-performance sports car, but today the average diesel family saloon is likely just as powerful. Where the S excels is the package it delivers. It's a car that won't mask your inadequacies, and it's a car that you have to drive in the truest sense of the word.

The exhaust doubles as a skid-plate on the S, so caution is advised over bumps!

4 Relative values
– which model for you?

First, we need to split those in the market for the V6 model from the V8S, because the V8 model commands higher asking prices. Anybody looking at the V8 for the soundtrack and 'fun-factor' of the car rather than outright performance should also consider a good V6 variant though, because there isn't a bad sounding S model, or one that fails to bring out a sense of occasion on a weekend roof-down drive.

The S-Series in its purest form: The S1. (A Bamber)

The **S1** (initially known simply as the 'S' or 280S) is the car that TVR designed the S to be. It is the most raw, least capable, and most poorly assembled variant. It's also the best value, the most mechanically simple, and it provides a brilliant soundtrack. No owner of a Ford Capri 2.8i or Sierra XR4i could guess that those cars share the same engine, such is the bellow, rasp and howl emitted from the tailpipes of an S1, followed up with addictive 'popping'

The noise created by 2.9-engined cars like this S2 is closer to a V8 'burble,' but with a lovely offbeat note. (B Stone)

and 'banging' on the overrun. Simple electronics and excellent value for money, but only 130-140bhp in the real world, and the engine is resistant to tuning. The Bosch K-Jetronic injection system can also be problematic to those unfamiliar with it.

The **S2** (aka 290S, though TVR never actually referred to them as such) is visually similar to the S1. Some chrome trim was added to the rubber bumpers along with new OZ 8-spoke alloy wheels to replace the 5-spoke types of the S1. The interior was virtually identical too, though most S2s added electric windows and an electric boot release. The rear suspension geometry was revised to reduce the 'squat' behaviour under load symptomatic of so many cars with the semi-trailing arm design, but the key difference is the engine; the 2.9 engine is generally an improvement over the 2.8. However, when it comes to the drive of these cars, an S1 can deliver as much enjoyment as an S2 (or, indeed, any S variant), so don't discount the earlier car. An S2 model will normally command a slight premium over the S1.

Martin Roberts has owned his pristine S3 for twenty years! (M Roberts)

This lovely red V8S is enjoying a run out. (P Hewitt)

The **S3** (or **S3C**, if it was fitted with catalytic converters), which replaced the S2, has more to consider. Once again, the rear suspension geometry was altered, this time by modifying the trailing arms to a toe-adjustable type. The increased length of the doors is probably the most notable advantage over the S1 and S2, and the S3 was the first model to feature these, along with the revised dashboard. Some models also received driving lamps under the front bumper, and most later examples also received the Citroën CX wing mirrors which adorned so many other specialised British cars of the era. S3s tend to command premiums over the S1 and S2 model, possibly in the region of 15-20% when the cars in question are in good condition.

The **V8S** model looks very much like the S3, though some later examples were fitted with the 5-spoke 'Imola' alloy wheel from the newer Chimaera. The bonnet lost the off-centre forward-facing scoop of previous V6 models in favour of a rearward-facing bulge, and all models benefitted from the Citroën door mirrors and front driving lamps. The slightly wider track affords the V8S a more aggressive stance and more assured handling. The rear brakes were upgraded to discs from the drums of the V6 models, and a limited-slip differential was installed. The exhaust tailpipes are larger bore and spaced further apart than the regular S design, but surprisingly the engine makes do with a smaller exhaust silencer, so the V8S model offers better ground clearance. As previously mentioned, V8S residuals tend to be significantly higher than those of the V6 models.

The last S ever built is Nigel Bromley's S4C. Finished in Starmist Green, it was once owned by Peter Wheeler's wife, Vicky.

The final incarnation of the S was the **S4C**. The Ford 2.9 V6 engine was back, lining up alongside the V8S, but most of the uprated chassis from the Rover V8-engined range topper was retained, along with the brakes, differential, and suspension. The bonnet was also a fresh design; completely devoid of any humps, it featured discreet vents along the inner edges. It's the ultimate V6-powered S-Series, and the rarest, which makes it difficult to value as they seldom come up for sale. Expect to pay anywhere between the price of an S3 and a V8S.

Should you find a car that's been through a full body off restoration, however, this will considerably affect the value. Aside from rust concerns, a full body off chassis restoration is desirable because many mechanical components will have also been renewed during the process. For example, an S1 or S2 with a recently refurbished chassis could command a higher asking price than an original S3.

A full body off chassis refurbishment should increase the market value of a car. (Southways Automotive Ltd)

5 Before you view
– be well informed

To avoid a wasted journey, and the disappointment of finding that the car doesn't match your expectations, it will help if you're very clear about the questions you want to ask before you pick up the phone. Some of these points might appear basic, but when you're excited about the prospect of buying your dream classic, it's amazing how some of the most obvious things slip the mind. Also, check the current values of the model you're interested in. Classic car magazines can provide a price guide and auction results.

Where is the car?
Is it going to be worth travelling to the next county/state, or even across a border? A locally advertised car, though it may not sound very interesting, can add to your knowledge for very little effort, and it might even be in better condition than expected.

Dealer or private sale
Establish early on if the car is being sold by its owner or by a trader. A private owner should have all the history, so don't be afraid to ask detailed questions. A dealer may have more limited knowledge of a car's history, but should have some documentation. A dealer may offer a warranty/guarantee (ask for a printed copy) and finance.

Cost of collection and delivery
A dealer may well be used to quoting for delivery by car transporter. A private owner may agree to meet you halfway, but only agree to this after you've seen the car at the vendor's address, to validate the documents. Or you could meet halfway and agree the sale, but insist on meeting at the vendor's address for the handover.

2.8 V6 engine (top) can be identified by the rectangular plenum, with single throttle body on the side; the 2.9's (bottom) is curved, with twin-throttle bodies. (www.myfavouritephotos.com)

View – when and where
It's always preferable to view at the vendor's home or business premises. In the case of a private sale, the car's documentation should tally with the vendor's name and address. Arrange to view only in daylight and avoid a wet day (most cars look better in poor light or when wet).

Reason for sale

Make it one of the first questions. Why is the car being sold and how long has it been with the current owner? How many previous owners?

Left-hand drive to right-hand drive/specials and convertibles

If a steering conversion has been done it can only reduce the value. It may well be that other aspects of the car still reflect the specification of a foreign market.

Condition (body/chassis/interior/mechanicals)

Ask for an honest appraisal of the car's condition. Ask specifically about some of the check items described in chapter 7.

All-original specification

An original equipment car is invariably of higher value than a customised version.

Matching data/legal ownership

Do VIN/chassis, engine numbers and licence plate match the official registration document? Is the owner's name and address recorded in the official registration documents?

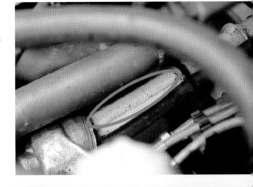

For those countries that require an annual test of roadworthiness, does the car have a document showing it complies (an MoT certificate in the UK, which can be verified on 0845 600 5977)?

If a smog/emissions certificate is mandatory, does the car have one?

If required, does the car carry a current road fund license/licence plate tag?

Does the vendor own the car outright? Money might be owed to a finance company or bank. The car could even be stolen. Several organisations will supply the data on ownership, based on the car's licence plate number, for a fee. Such companies can often also tell you whether the car has been 'written-off' by an insurance company. In the UK, these organisations can supply vehicle data:

HPI – 01722 422 422
AA – 0870 600 0836
DVLA – 0870 240 0010
RAC – 0870 533 3660

Other countries will have similar organisations.

Unleaded fuel

If necessary, has the car been modified to run on unleaded fuel?

Check that these two correspond, because the chassis – not the body – is the ID of the car!

Insurance
Check with your existing insurer before setting out. Your current policy might not cover you to drive the car.

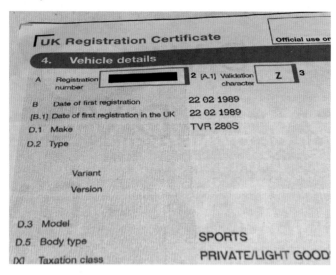

Make: TVR280S
Model: (blank!)
Registration anomalies like these create problems when using on-line, registration number-based services such as HPI reports.

How you can pay
A cheque/check will take several days to clear, and the seller may prefer to sell to a cash buyer. A banker's draft (a cheque issued by a bank) is as good as cash, but safer, so contact your own bank and become familiar with the formalities that are necessary to obtain one.

Buying at auction?
If the intention is to buy at auction, see chapter 10 for further advice.

Professional vehicle check (mechanical examination)
There are often marque/model specialists who will undertake professional examination of a vehicle on your behalf. Owners' clubs will be able to put you in touch with such specialists.
Other organisations that will carry out a general professional check in the UK are:
• AA – 0800 085 3007 (motoring organisation with vehicle inspectors)
• ABS – 0800 358 5855 (specialist vehicle inspection company)
• RAC – 0870 533 3660 (motoring organisation with vehicle inspectors)
Other countries will have similar organisations.

6 Inspection equipment
– these items will really help

This book
Reading glasses (if you need them for close work)
Torch
Probe (a small screwdriver works very well)
Overalls
Mirror on a stick
Digital camera
A friend, preferably a knowledgeable enthusiast

Before you rush out of the door, gather together a few items that will help as you work your way around the car. This book is designed to be your guide at every step, so take it along and use the check boxes to help you assess each area of the car you're interested in. Don't be afraid to let the seller see you using it.

Take your reading glasses if you need them to read documents and make close up inspections.

A torch with fresh batteries will be useful for peering into the wheelarches and under the car.

A small screwdriver can be used – with care – as a probe to inspect the condition of the metal chassis, particularly in the wheelarches and on the underside. With this you should be able to check an area of severe corrosion, but be careful – if it's really bad the screwdriver might go right through the tube!

Be prepared to get dirty. Take along a pair of overalls, if you have them. Fixing a mirror at an angle on the end of a stick may seem odd, but you'll probably need it to check the condition of the underside of the car. It will also help you to peer into some of the important crevices. You can also use it, together with the torch, along the underside of the sills, and on the floor.

If you have a digital camera, take it along so that later you can study some areas of the car more closely. Take a picture of any part of the car that causes you concern, and seek a friend's opinion.

Ideally, have a friend or knowledgeable enthusiast accompany you – a second opinion is always valuable.

7 Fifteen minute evaluation
– walk away or stay?

Though most S-Series look alike, the manner in which they behave can differ between examples. The aim of this chapter is to establish whether it's worth staying to inspect a car further, or whether to walk away and wait for a better car to become available.

Nigel Salmon's red S1 opened up and ready for inspection.

The most important part of the car to inspect is the tubular steel chassis. This is more critical than the way the car looks, drives and sounds, because everything that makes the car what it is is bolted to this. It's often said that there are two types of TVR: cars that have had the chassis 'done,' and cars that need it!

For the purpose of a quick inspection, we'll treat the chassis as the 'map' and follow it around the car. The chassis comprises a transmission tunnel acting as a spine. Comprising two lower rectangular rails and two upper round tube rails running front to back, it's interlinked by a number of diagonal smaller

Not the most exciting place to start, but the chassis is the area you should be paying the most attention to. (Southways Automotive Ltd)

tubes and braces to give it strength and rigidity. The engine, gearbox, propshaft and differential sit within this structure; the driver and passenger sit either side. At the front, suspension wishbones are attached to the upper and lower chassis rails. Inspect these wishbones for corrosion as they're not available off-the-shelf, so used parts, repair or even fabrication are your only options here. Also inspect the suspension dampers all round (including bushes), as reconditioning or replacement can be costly.

Paul Hewitt's red V8S undergoing recommissioning after a chassis restoration. (Southways Automotive Ltd)

At the front of the chassis are two short square tubes, to which the bonnet hinges are fixed. Any distortion to these tubes indicates the car may have been involved in a frontal impact. The radiator – mounted at an angle in either two 'blade' mounts (early cars) or a single bolt-on frame (later cars) – is worth checking as replacements are not cheap! The cooling fan is a single design, and was mounted on both the front and the rear of the radiator over the course of production. Also examine the coolant hoses and metal coolant pipes in the engine bay. Silicone/stainless replacements are available, but factor in the costs, as original rubber hoses won't have much life left in them by now.

Continuing rearward, the transmission tunnel runs up to the fuel tank. The tank itself is made of mild steel, and though replacements are available, they can be costly. It's bolted to a cradle, which in turn is bolted to the end of the chassis, and also supports the rearmost section of the body tub.

As the entire front portion of the body is made up of the bonnet (hood), the remainder of the body tub is supported by the 'outriggers,' pictured here. (Southways Automotive Ltd)

Any repairs that have been carried out here need to be treated with the same caution as rusty holes, until the quality of the repair is proven. (Southways Automotive Ltd)

The outriggers are a series of tubes that protrude outward from the lower chassis rails on both sides of the car and form a 'sill' along the wheelbase of the car. Corrosion-wise, the front tube is the most vulnerable area on the chassis, but the rear beam is the most important, as it is home not only to the seatbelt mechanisms, but also the rear suspension trailing arms. Aside from the damper mounts, this is the only place the rear suspension attaches to the chassis, so it's critical the chassis is structurally solid in this area. It's one of the hardest sections to repair too (even for an experienced welder) due to the poor access afforded by both the bracket shape and the positioning of them relative to the body.

Many people struggle working out where exactly to place a jack under the S chassis (for the record, going in from the front and spreading the load across the two lower chassis rails is ideal, while at the rear the lower beam directly under the turret area will be strong enough to use a single trolley jack), so keep a keen eye out for damaged tubes as well as rust". Don't be afraid to ask the seller if you can carefully poke any questionable areas of the chassis with a screwdriver or similar device; if they've told you the chassis is structurally solid, they have nothing to fear!

We'll cover the chassis in more detail in chapter nine, so assuming you've found no horror stories underneath the car, spend some time looking at it, and inside it.

The biggest thing to concern yourself with bodywork on a TVR S-Series (besides the normal paint issues) is panel alignment. With the S, the biggest problem is that many of the panels never actually fitted perfectly from new. It's a problem that is more commonly found on the earlier cars, because the build quality improved as the years of production passed. It isn't solely limited to the early cars though, so pay particular attention to:

Bonnet (hood)
The bonnet on an S is difficult to align nicely, so you'll likely encounter a car with poor shutlines. What you need to establish is whether they could be adjusted to fit better, because in some cases the bonnets just don't fit properly. Look at the shutlines on one side of the car, then the other. If the bonnet is sitting too far outboard of the wing on one side, is it sitting too far inboard on the other side? If so, then you could likely improve it, but if it's a mirror image you're unlikely to be able to.

This S1's bonnet fit – though reasonably good by the usual standard – stands little chance of improvement without body alteration.

Doors
The three edges of the door that meet the body need to be flush. For example, if the leading edge is sitting proud of the A-pillar, and the trailing edge is proud of the B-pillar, then the lower edge of the door needs to be the same, or you won't be able to adjust one without affecting the other. Also check that the doors aren't fouling on the inside of the B-pillar aperture. If the panel gap is too tight, the doors can rub through the paint

The odds of finding a perfectly fitting door on an S are slim. This S1's offering is a good effort, especially for an early car.

when opening and closing. This could just be poor alignment of the doors, or poor alignment of the whole body-tub! Or, it could be …

Dropped doors
One of the biggest issues with the S-Series, dropped doors are both common and difficult to rectify. The doors are a GRP moulding fixed on to an upper and lower purpose-made steel bracket. These brackets (and, in turn, the doors) rotate on a nylon bush in the centre, through which an M10 bolt (or M8, if the car is a very early S1) passes until it fastens into a brass bobbin located in the GRP at top and bottom. Open the doors, gently lifting them upwards by the handle when they're about a third of the way open. You might detect a very small amount of play, but what you don't want to find is any more than 5mm of movement up and down. There are three possible causes in the event you do: if you're lucky, it'll be a loose fixing (the M10 bolt, normally) or a worn nylon guide bush (the ones located in the steel brackets). However, if you're less fortunate, it'll be the upper brass bobbin breaking out of the GRP. Simply glassing it back into place is difficult – haggle accordingly or walk away.

Open both doors and check for up and down play in the top hinge attachment. Brass bobbins breaking out of the bodywork is a common fault, and not a simple fix. (Southways Automotive Ltd)

Roof
Two areas to concern yourself with: Firstly, the targa roof panels; do they sit flush? Secondly, check that the door windows clear the fold-down roof section once it's fixed upright. They need to clear the roof frame comfortably and evenly – if they touch it's not unknown for windows to smash if the door is shut with the window up. While you're there, check the condition of the roof fabric and the rear screen; particularly around the roof struts, as they have a tendency to hole.

Targa panel design means that one side overlaps the other, but both need to sit as flush as possible when secured in place.

Finish with the bodywork by looking for crazes or cracking in the GRP, especially on the doors and the rear ¼ panels. The S can pick up stone chipping on the bonnet and along the 'sill' areas, where the wheels have flicked debris and grit at the body over the years. Remember that GRP-bodied cars can be more labour-intensive, so a repair cost for a seemingly small blemish could be more than you think.

Lastly, look at the interior in closer detail. A leaky roof can cause all manner of smells inside, so trust your nose! Rainwater tends to congregate in the footwells, and down the back of the seats, so tip them forwards and have a look for damp. Leaks cause corrosion issues with the seatbelts and seat runner mechanisms, so check that the seats slide cleanly. The seats themselves are normally half-hide, or in rare cases full-leather. Tailor-made replacement seat covers are available, but will cost around ●x600 for the parts. Full carpet sets can be obtained in the event that yours are faded or damaged. Budget another ●x700 for the kit; more if you don't want to attempt fitting it yourself.

Cracking and crazing is a common issue. This external wound was inflicted by an unsecured spare wheel in the boot.

The dashboard, which 90% of the time is trimmed in a matching vinyl/leather, is the most difficult repair. If this is damaged, you'll need to factor in repair costs of at least ●x1000 if you want to have it put right at a trimmers.

There is clearly more to a TVR S-Series than simply the chassis, body and interior, but these three areas are the most costly to rectify. If the car in question is at the top of the price range, they all need to be in good order. If you're willing to attend to any areas that need work yourself, then this needs to be reflected in the price of the car early on.

The Mulberry dashboard of the author's late S1.

The goal here is to buy a TVR S that won't financially assault you in the near future!

"Chassis, chassis and chassis" – in ownership circles, this is common advice for any potential buyer, and it's completely accurate. Yes, rust is an issue, but it's not just corrosion you need to worry about. Everything is bolted to the chassis, and the possibility that repair bills will begin to snowball should you decide to take on a rusty chassis is very real.

Just because a chassis has been 'repaired,' doesn't give it the green light. Poor repairs can equate to the same thing as rust, because they'll need sorting out too.

Condition is the most important thing. Too many people end up with a troublesome car because they preferred the colour of the piping on the carpet (or something equally daft). Obviously you need to want the car in question, but condition is paramount.

These are more labour intensive cars to work on than the majority of mass-produced offerings. A few small jobs could add up to a four-figure bill! Ask yourself if you could have bought a better one had you put that money towards the purchase rather than the repair work.

Savings – put some money aside. Your S-Series WILL need something putting right shortly after purchase. Not as a result of foul play on the part of the seller, it's just highly likely that you (or your specialist workshop of choice) will spot an issue that the seller knew nothing about.

The chassis is rusty, but the dampers are also tired, the bushes perished, and the brake and fuel lines are corroded. Beware of snowballing costs! (Southways Automotive Ltd)

You have to wonder whether the rust that was replaced here was stronger than what replaced it. (Southways Automotive Ltd)

So, you've decided to take a closer look at your prospective S-Series. Time to go looking for trouble!

Body (general issues)

Though scratches and cracks can appear anywhere, pay particular attention to the windscreen surround and surrounding areas, and along the 'sill' area. Check also for signs of scrapes or scuffs along the base of the door, as the relatively low height of the door can lead to contact with kerbs. Check the entire surface of the bonnet for crazing or cracking, especially in the areas above the striker pins, as well as the area directly above the battery (on V6 models). The recess below the rear number plate is also an area susceptible to surface cracks, and the boot aperture can be damaged by people trying to place the roof panels in the boot. Lastly, check the bodywork either side of the boot for crazing and cracks in the GRP, as heavy items placed loosely in the boot can damage the bodywork from the inside.

Doors

Are the doors flush-fitting? Are the panel gaps even? The door should open and close freely, without catching the bodywork in the aperture or resting on the kickplate/sill. With your hand keeping the exterior handle open, press the door shut and then open again a few times. If the door feels like it 'bumps' up as the lock mechanism meets the striker, it could be a sign that either the striker needs adjusting, or that the door is dropping. With the door slightly open, gently lift the door by the handle to check for any free play. If you detect any, it's cause to look further and try to decipher whether it's simply the bushing (not as serious), or the mount in the bodywork at fault. This can be observed more closely by checking to see if the top mounting bolt is moving with the door, or whether the door is moving, with the bolt remaining still. If the bolt is moving, it's either loose (if you're lucky) or a failing mounting bobbin – if it's the latter haggle accordingly because this is not an easy fix.

Doors. One of the S's notorious weak points, both in terms of the strength of the mountings and fit and finish. (Southways Automotive Ltd)

Door mirrors   ④ ③ ② ①

The majority of S-Series will be fitted with one of two factory options. They are: the 'bunny ear,' as fitted to earlier models, and the Citroën CX units, as fitted to later models. The earlier types offer abysmal visibility, but they're very simple and seldom fail. The CX mirrors, on the other hand, cannot be installed to the door as Citroën intended for the CX, so they have to be installed after assembly, which sometimes results in ill-fitting mirrors. Furthermore, the S-Series is the type of car that's usually stowed in a garage while not in use, and might have its mirrors continually folded in and out far more than would have been expected of the average 1980s French saloon. As a result, the metal bracket connecting the mirror body to the door can fracture, and replacement is a fairly involved job. It's not a reason to walk away from a car, but check that the mirrors aren't 'drooping,' and the glass is secure.

Door windows   ④ ③ ② ①

Most S-Series will have electric windows, but these can be slow in operation due to tired motors, poor alignment, wiring issues, or all three combined. Check that the dropglass slides up and down freely, and that the pane is free of scratches. Check also that the glass does not foul the roof hoop when erected and, with the window halfway up, check the glass doesn't rattle in the door: a sign that the window channel rubbers or regulator mountings may be failing. Check this again with the window fully up, and listen out for such noises on the test drive. The rubber seal at the base of the targa panels is notoriously poor at making a good seal with the top of the window, so inspect it for gaps or signs of failure.

Bonnet (hood)   ④ ③ ② ①

On all but the earliest S1 models (also known as twin-bonnet pull cars), the bonnet release lever is a thin bar, located to the immediate left of the steering column (confusingly, on cars with mechanical boot release, the original Ford red bonnet release handle operates the boot). Pull the lever towards you, and the bonnet should pop up enthusiastically and evenly on both sides of the car. Anything else may just be a case of poor adjustment of the lock pins or bonnet, but could also be worn lock mechanisms, and these aren't easy to replace. Check the 'blade' in the lock mechanism is still nicely sprung, and not seized

The bonnet can be troublesome on an S, so check alignment, lock operation, and condition of the mountings.

or jammed, and also that the striker on the bonnet is mounted securely, and that no signs of stress failure can be observed in the mounting plate. Upon opening the bonnet, you'll find a surprising lack of access to the engine bay, thanks to the bonnet's low opening angle. Check for damage along the lower grill opening, where the underside often makes contact with the ground, and also for play or signs of failure to the hinge assemblies. The hinges fix into two-square tubes at the extreme front of the chassis; check these aren't misshapen or damaged, and show no signs of poor quality welding. The opposing side of the hinges are affixed to two plywood panels, glassed on the underside of the bonnet, either side of the radiator. Check these for rot or damage.

Windscreen delamination

An annoying niggle on any car, but on a TVR S it's compounded by the fact that the windscreens are not only difficult to source, but also difficult to fit. It's quite common to find black insulation tape over the edges of a screen to hide delamination.

Roof

Check the roof fabric for rips and tears. The most vulnerable areas are the leading edges and the section down the side of the roof hoop, approaching the hinge. It's also worth inspecting for poor quality stitching around the rear screen, and signs of moss or staining along the base of the roof. There are also two locating tabs on the front and rear edge of

Windscreen delamination: not cause to walk away from a potential purchase, but don't assume it'll be a straightforward rectification.

each targa panel, which should locate cleanly into receptacles in the bodywork and roof hoop; check these aren't damaged, or loose. Ideally, the targa panels will sit completely flush with the windscreen surround, the roof hoop, and each other. The roof hoop is anchored by a bolt at the base on each side which can work loose, and access to any loose fixings will often require peeling away leather or vinyl. I'd also advise conducting some of your test drive with the roof on, so you can listen out for any squeaks or rattles from it. When you stop to remove the roof, ask the seller to show you how it's done – the care they put into it is telling of their level of mechanical sympathy. It's worth pointing out that if you view a car in cold weather, the seller may be reluctant to fold down the roof for fear of damaging the rear screen.

Inspect the locating tabs on the targa roof panels, along with the receiving slots in the bodywork and roof.

Seats & upholstery ④ ③ ② ①

The trimming and upholstering in the S-Series was originally of a good quality from the factory, but maintenance of the materials used is vital to prolonging the life of the interior, so check that the leather of the seats is still supple and free from cracking. With the earlier 'wraparound' dashboard, the entire dash and centre-console are all one piece, so check the condition of the vinyl trim carefully, as any repairs may require the removal of the entire dashboard. The later dash design is two-piece, with a removable console. Removal of the dash itself is still a time-consuming affair, so check the wood veneer is also in good condition and free of cracks or signs of lifting (some cars have vinyl, or a metal panel, painted brown with black marks, to resemble wood). Sit in both seats and check that they slide back and forth smoothly, as reluctance may point to corrosion in the runners, caused by possible water ingress. Also, check that the backrests adjust smoothly via the lever at the base of the seat and lock into place securely, and that the plastic trim that covers the lever mechanism is secure and not broken. Tip the seat forwards and examine the rear of the seat for wear or damage. Some cars featured piped edges, which was stitched into the seat bases and backrest. It's vulnerable to the movement of backs and bottoms, so check for damage along the edges.

Gauges/switchgear ④ ③ ② ①

TVR used their own instruments so, with the exception of the analogue clock, any gauge not proudly displaying the 'TVR' logo isn't original. Check that all instruments function correctly, as replacements are not always easy to find. In particular, the speedometer on S2 models onwards is electronically-driven, and the sender units for these can be difficult to source and very tricky to access on the V8S. The column stalks and switches are Ford-based, but check the bank of tell-tale warning lights, which are located in an 'arc' following the curve of the dash from the speedo towards the radio, or on later models, directly in front of the driver. Not only are the original black lenses impossible to buy new, some of the lamps require the removal of the entire panel to replace a bulb! The instruments should illuminate with the activation of the sidelights, and through a rotary dial there are three possible intensities (often referred to as dim, very dim and off by owners). It's also worth advising that the voltage-gauge will probably be underreading, and that you should not trust the fuel gauge until you *know* where empty is relative to its readings (I've run out of petrol with an indicated ¼ of a tank in an S).

Electrics ④ ③ ② ①

A GRP-bodied car doesn't possess a natural earth, so all circuits have to be earthed onto the chassis. This means a lot of additional wiring, which increases the likelihood of problems. It also means that any DIY-approaches to repairs or accessories should be inspected more closely than with a metal-bodied car. The wiring loom connections to the bonnet (for headlamps, indicators etc) are susceptible to corrosion due to their location. TVRs often suffer from power drains, so if battery charge or jump start connectors are visible, ask some questions; all S-Series are simple cars electronically, so if a battery keeps going flat, it suggests wiring problems.

Alternator/charging circuit ④ ③ ② ①

Due to an anomaly in the design, on V6 models the battery charge lamp may not extinguish until the engine first exceeds idle speed (sometimes 2500rpm is needed).

The voltage gauge will probably not give a reliable reading either, so it might be worth taking a multi-meter and confirming that the battery charge is at least 13.5v, rising to around 14.2v at fast idle. In isolation, a worn alternator isn't a big problem, but the symptoms of poor wiring could be masked as an alternator fault.

Heating & ventilation
A component worth checking, because replacement of the blower motor sometimes necessitates removal of the dashboard. Check that it provides a good flow of air to the windscreen, and that it switches to the lower vents via the slider control. Check also that it operates at the different speed positions on the rotary switch. The circular vents at either end of the dashboard (early dashes) or in the centre console above the radio (later models) are fresh-air vents, ducted by flexi pipes running from the bonnet through the engine bay (in the case of some later models, the left-hand vent is routed from above the gearbox). Check that these ducting hoses are intact and not holed. It's not an expensive fix if they are, but you could be inhaling fumes from the engine bay!

Cooling system
In addition to the radiator, there is an alloy swirl pot and a plastic expansion tank. Both of these have a removable cap, and (for reference) the correct positioning is the pressure cap on the swirl pot, and the sealed cap on the expansion tank. Be careful when removing and refitting the cap to the swirl pot as the collar often wears, causing the cap to lose purchase and release itself at the slightest touch, even when tightening. The V6 cars use an all-iron engine, so regular coolant changes are critical to prevent any build-up of corrosion and possible restriction of waterways, and while the V8 is an all-alloy affair, you should also check that the coolant has been changed regularly. The original radiators are copper core items, so inspect it for corrosion, damage and evidence of leaks. Check all coolant hoses for signs of deterioration, swelling, or impending failure, and all steel coolant pipes for corrosion. Lastly, check that the coolant fan cuts in, brings the temperature down, and cuts out again; a fan staying on constantly suggests poor circulation, and it shouldn't come on at all while driving.

Some cars will have been upgraded with an alloy radiator, which is a relatively costly undertaking. (Southways Automotive Ltd)

Servo & brake/clutch hydraulics

Obviously the standard checks apply here, but there are a couple of areas that specifically apply to the S that you should be aware of. Firstly, the brake servo has a tendency to rot on the underside, so try to feel around the seam of the unit for any holes or corrosion. A leaky servo will present you with a very firm pedal combined with a lack of braking effort. Earlier models had a remote fluid reservoir mounted on the bulkhead, but many will have been retrofitted with the later unit mounted atop the brake master cylinder. The other area to inspect is the front brake hoses; originally the S used a flexi-hose arrangement from the chassis to the suspension upright, then a jumper brake pipe fixed to the upright, which kept the flexi hose away from the suspension coil spring during moments of full articulation, and then a second flexi hose from the jumper pipe to the brake caliper. Some cars will have been fitted with a single-length hose from chassis directly to the caliper, and if the hose length isn't spot-on, it can occasionally foul the suspension spring.

Rotten brake servos are very common on the S, so feel all around the servo unit; especially the bottom seam. (Southways Automotive Ltd)

Steering

For many, the steering is one of the best aspects of the S. Check the inner tie rods for any play as they enter the rack. These aren't always replaceable, and your only option is a full refurb as the original racks (of which there are a couple of variations) aren't available. Inspect the mounting bushes for signs of perishing, and check also for play at the pinion shaft, the upper and lower universal joints on the lower part of the steering column, and the bulkhead bearing, which is accessible in the driver's wheelarch. On the test drive, it should track straight and true, with a reasonable amount of self-centre action.

Suspension bushes

4 3 2 1

These bushes dramatically affect the handling and responsiveness of the car. Any signs of perishing can cause play, which will negatively affect the geometry of the car's suspension and steering in certain conditions. Consider also that the cost to refresh all the suspension bushes is not always the whole story; the fixing bolts sometimes rust into the bush sleeves, so removal can involve cutting the arms away. In the event that you do successfully remove all the suspension arms, you might also find that they're rusty. What started as a suspension bush change is now six rusted suspension arms, some of which may need repairing.

Perished bushes will negatively affect the drive of the car, and can be costly to replace. (Southways Automotive Ltd)

That's the line of thinking you need to take with most things fixed to the chassis: "what else will I need to fix while I'm there?" Lastly, some cars may have been fitted with polyurethane upgraded bushes, and while these can sometimes lead to an increase of NVH (noise vibration harshness) on many production cars, I haven't found this to be the case on the S (or any other TVR) as the original bushes are also on the 'stiff' side, so don't be put off by a car fitted with poly-bushes, as long as you like the way it drives.

Dampers (shock-absorbers)/ride height

4 3 2 1

It's worth checking the bushes at the top and bottom of the strut, as per the suspension arms, as these can perish and cause excessive play. Most S-Series were originally fitted with Koni dampers, which had a red body, but the chances are they'll have been replaced by now, normally with items that are adjustable for ride height, damping, or both. If the car seems to be sitting excessively low, check for damage to the exhaust silencer. If the car is fitted with adjustable dampers, but rides poorly or doesn't handle terribly well, it may need adjustment. In order to do that, check that the spring seats aren't rusted, and that the damping adjuster wheels move freely.

Just because it has adjustable dampers (shock-absorbers) fitted, doesn't mean it won't need new units at some point. (Southways Automotive Ltd)

Wheels

Typically, there are three main types of alloy wheel you'll find on an S-Series. All were 7Jx15in, unlike later TVRs which used staggered sizes. S1 models featured a 5-spoke 'slot' style rim, while the S2 brought with it an 8-spoke deep-dish version from OZ, which was carried through to the last S4C models. Both of these designs used a diamond-cut finish, with the early wheels using grey detailing inside the spokes and centres, and the 8-spokes using black. Inspect the wheels for signs of corrosion, because although diamond-cutting provides a very aesthetically pleasing finish, it's not very durable. It's also quite expensive to have carried out, and if the corrosion is severe, the resultant pitting may be so deep that it won't be possible to eradicate it. The third design of wheel was the 'Imola' 5-spokes, as fitted to the front of most Chimaera models. These were painted silver from new, and as a result are much more durable, if not quite as attractive. Many owners deem the diamond-cut finish to be too delicate, or are forced by deep corrosion to have the original 5 or 8-spoke wheels powder-coated too. Whether you like that finish look or not is a purely subjective matter, but be aware that you may not be able to revert back to diamond-cut if corrosion was the deciding factor. Bear in mind that if a car doesn't have the original style wheel, it may not be easy to find a replacement set if you want the original look.

Top: Original 5-spoke S1 alloys. Centre: 8-spoke versions fitted to all other variants. Bottom: Optional 'Imola' 5-spoke design, borrowed from newer Chimaera. (www.myfavouritephotos.com)

Tyres

The S is of an era when its size of 205/60R15 was the go-to choice for performance cars. Today, these tyres are considered an oddball size, though fortunately they're still available. What you need to be aware of is that all S-Series used a 'V' speed-rated tyre (up to 149mph). In the event that the car you're looking at is wearing H-rated tyres, you may need to renew all four to comply with your insurance policy. Though not all non-premium branded tyres are bad, the choice of tyre fitted to a car during its life is an indication of how much an owner was willing to spend to look after their car. Bridgestone tyres were originally fitted, and are still a

Tyre date stamp.

good choice today, along with Dunlop and Uniroyal. Check the date stamp on the rubber though (see image), as these cars don't tend to cover many miles annually, so the tyres often degrade before they run out of tread. Lastly, check the condition of the tread itself, as many tyre-shops do not have the settings for these cars, so just revert to 'neutral.' It's normal to have slightly more wear on the inner edges than the outer edges.

Engine (Ford V6)

There hasn't been much mention of engines in this book so far, and for good reason! While no technological marvel, the 'Cologne' V6 engine is a durable overhead-valve unit, and rarely gives serious trouble. All versions are on the 'tappy' side when it comes to valvetrain noise, but check the noise isn't excessive (or that it's not an exhaust leak masquerading as noisy tappets). The 2.8 version used a timing gear to drive the camshaft, while the 2.9 used a conventional chain, so listen for tell-tale rattles. Some 2.9 engines also featured hydraulic lifters, but many also used conventional adjustable types. Otherwise it's business as usual, though check for excessive smoke at start-up and on the move, leaky gaskets, and flat spots in the rev range, which may signal issues with the injection system. It's also worth looking for failing head gaskets; corrosion can quickly build up in the cooling system due to the engine's all-iron properties, and many owners don't change the coolant as regularly as they should. One way to test for this is to start the engine cold, run it for 40-50 seconds, and then shut it down again. Then immediately remove the pressure cap from the swirl pot; if coolant immediately pushes its way out, that's a sign that the cooling system is being pressurised by the combustion chambers. Please note: Don't do this when the engine is anything other than cold!

The Ford 'Cologne' engine – if not a spectacular performer – is tough, has bags of character, and will put a smile on your face. (Southways Automotive Ltd)

Engine (Rover V8)

4 3 2 1

Like the 'Cologne,' the Rover V8 is a strong yet simple affair, albeit slightly more advanced with its use of aluminium over cast iron. Head gasket issues are still worth keeping an eye out for, particularly as the cylinder liners can get dislodged inside the block as a result of overheating, causing compression issues. The Rover V8 uses hydraulic lifters, and any tapping sounds could be a sign of failed lifter(s) or broken rocker pad(s) operating on a valve. The fact it uses hydraulic lifters can also mask camshaft wear, which is common on most Rover variants, and affects the 3.9 at the 70,000-100,000 mile mark, depending on how strictly it's been maintained. A lack of power above 4500rpm is a common symptom of this. The 'RV8' suffers oil leaks (as does the 'Cologne'), especially around the sump area. The key to living a stress-free life with the engine in a TVR S-Series is previous maintenance; if previous owners have kept on top of problems as they arise, you'd be very unlucky to suffer any serious engine problems in the future.

The iconic Rover V8 engine turns the S into a more serious performer, albeit at a price. (Southways Automotive Ltd)

Intake bellows and general running (2.8)

4 3 2 1

One for the S1 alone: The mechanical K-Jetronic fuel-injection system of the 2.8 engine is almost entirely vacuum-metered, and as a result, any leaks or perforations in rubber hoses or bellows can cause all manner of issues with starting, idling, or high-load fuel demand. Check the condition of the rubber intake bellows mounted to the top of the fuel-metering unit above the air filter box; if leaks are present, it won't run properly, so ensure it's behaving properly from cold all the way up to operating temperature.

The rubber intake bellows on the 2.8 can cause running issues if perforated.

Leaking sump pan (oilpan) & exhaust damage

4 3 2 1

The exhaust is worthy of inspection, as replacements can be costly. On the V6 especially, the main silencer hangs much lower under the car than any other component. A further problem confined to the V6 models is the way it passes directly underneath the sump; a pair of clamps seal the main section of the exhaust to the front downpipes directly under the sump pan, but there is little clearance between sump and clamp. Repeated impact from below the exhaust can result in the clamp puncturing the sump, so if the sump is very oily, be aware that it might not just be a gasket. To compound the issue further on a V6, if a leak is spotted and it *is* simply the gasket, removing the sump with the engine in-situ is not possible, due to the chassis

Thoughtful positioning of the exhaust clamps on the V6 models is required to prevent percussion damage like this to the sump. (Southways Automotive Ltd)

brace that passes underneath. Some people will have modified the chassis to allow sump removal – with varying degrees of professionalism – but most cars will be as they were originally, so an oil leak can turn into an engine-out job.

Exhaust manifolds/headers

4 3 2 1

Any S can suffer with leaks from the exhaust joints at the engine, which can either be due to failed gaskets, or worse, a failed manifold/header. The 2.8 models use an original Ford Cortina/Taunus cast iron manifold (mounted backwards), and these are now at an age where they're very delicate. Replacements are also very difficult to source. Even if only the gaskets are leaking, the manifold is very unlikely to be removed from the engine in one piece, potentially rendering it scrap. A stainless tubular replacement is available, but costly. The 2.9 and V8S used TVR's own tubular steel headers, and although renewing blown gaskets is likely to yield more successful results, the headers themselves can crack around all the welded areas. It's worth listening for leaks, particularly on the test drive, so select a higher gear than you normally would and try accelerating hard from 30mph; a 'tapping' sound in sync with the engine revolutions may indicate a leak.

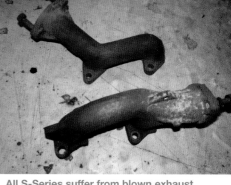

All S-Series suffer from blown exhaust manifold gaskets, but the manifolds themselves can fracture, too, especially the cast iron components of the 2.8 engines. (Southways Automotive Ltd)

Engine mounts ④ ③ ② ①
Engine mounts are a difficult engine component to change in any S-Series, due to poor access, particularly on the V6 model. Ensure their health by examining the clearance between the anti-roll bar and the engine sump pan. There should be approximately 8mm at least, and any less indicates that the engine mounts may be sagging, or even incorrectly sized. Some owners try to pack washers under worn mounts in a bid to clear the sump of contact, and contact between the two is a bad situation, as the anti-roll bar can wear through the sump pan.

Ensure there is decent clearance between roll-bar and sump pan, otherwise the engine mounts may need changing. (Southways Automotive Ltd)

Clutch ④ ③ ② ①
Its action should be smooth, if not exactly 'light.' Typically, a clutch will last around 60-80k miles in the V6 models, and around 50-70k miles in the V8. The reason you need to be sure the clutch is in good order is that in all models it's a complete engine-out job, as it isn't possible to remove the gearbox from the engine within the confines of the chassis. There's also nowhere to rest your left leg in an S, so some drivers use the clutch pedal as a footrest. This damages the clutch release bearing, which is not designed to be operated under load for long periods of time. In the event the transmission seems to 'rumble,' 'squeal' or 'tick' excessively with the engine at idle and the car stationary, rest your foot on the clutch pedal and apply a tiny amount of pressure. If the noise disappears instantly, it's likely to be the release bearing (which is effectively going to mean changing the clutch anyway). If the noise persists, but fades away as you fully depress the clutch, it could be a sign of gearbox problems, though it should be noted that a small amount of mechanical noise is normal. Lastly, check that the clutch shows no signs of 'judder,' both when pulling away forwards and in reverse. Check for this before the test drive, during and after, because clutch judder is often

temperature dependent. There should be no judder at all, and its presence suggests a contaminated clutch plate, or glazed flywheel. A worn gearbox mounting can also exacerbate the issue.

Transmission   4   3   2   1

All S-Series were fitted with 5-speed all-synchromesh gearboxes, being either Ford's 'Type-9' (if mated to the blue oval's V6) or Rover's LT77 (when concerning the V8). Both are generally dependable, and both have the same standard shift-pattern, with 5th out at the top right of the gate, and reverse at the top left. The Ford gearbox has no oil drain plug, so there is a chance its oil is in poor condition – ask about the service records. Check there is no grinding when changing into 2nd and 3rd gear in either box, and that the boxes are relatively quiet in neutral at tickover with your foot off the clutch. The gearlever fitted to the V6 box is cranked to cater for the fact the selector is effectively underneath your elbow, and as a result moves through a rather odd arc that takes some getting used to. The shift is quite 'vague,' and though a degree of play is normal, excessive freeplay in the gate could lead to a worn selector bush, though this is a relatively easy fix. The lever in the V8 has a much shorter 'crank' and shouldn't exhibit any signs of sloppiness. If present, it's normally down to worn remote shifter housing bushes, which are a bit more involved to replace in-situ, though the spring tension on the lever mechanism is adjustable, and I often see cars which are not setup for optimum operation. Lastly, check underneath for oil leaks. Both the Ford and Rover engines are quite leaky by nature, but excessive leaking from the gearbox might require removal, which in turn would require removal of the engine.

Differential   4   3   2   1

Whether Ford V6 or Rover V8 powered, a Ford Sierra/Granada differential is fitted to all TVR S-Series. It's a reliable unit, and rarely gives any trouble, though it should be noted that, like the Ford gearbox, it doesn't have a drain plug, so the oil inside could need changing. S1, S2 and S3 models use a conventional 'open' differential, while V8S and S4C models make use of a viscous limited-slip variant. In reality, you won't feel the effects of this unless you begin driving in a manner that will make the seller upset, but it's worth getting into a car park and manoeuvring on full lock in both directions to listen for 'thumping' or clicking noises. A tired S diff is at its noisiest when under load in a high gear. Don't expect a silent diff (there's no soundproofing, and it's just behind you), but excessive whining may point to a problem.

Fuel tank & hoses   4   3   2   1

The fuel tank from the factory was steel, and can rust both inside and out, though aluminium and stainless replacements are available. If you're presented with a rusty tank, consider that if the internals are rusty too, there is a chance of a partially blocked pre-filter in the sump of the tank. While the car might run happily to start with, listen for 'gargling' noises, or changes in the pitch of the fuel pump. Blockages in fuel supply don't always make themselves known straight away.

Also check the condition of all the rubber fuel lines. Some of these hoses may be as old as the car, and a rupture while containing 3.0bar (43.5PSI) of fuel pressure onto a hot exhaust is a recipe for disaster. Renewal can often be an involved job, too.

If the fuel tank is rusty on the outside, it could also be rusty on the inside. (Southways Automotive Ltd)

Test drive

All S-Series will drive slightly differently, but you'll have no frame of reference unless you drive lots of different S-Series, so concern yourself with whether or not you like the one you're in, even if you're only buying it as a project; the more you drive it, the more you'll discover what's in need of repair!

Sitting in the car, the seats should be supple, and you should be able to feel at home right away. The clutch should release smoothly, with no judder. You'll need to be fairly delicate with throttle inputs in the V8 in particular, as the merest twitch of the foot can result in a lunge forward!

There's little point in me trying to describe to you exactly how you should interpret the car on the move, because they're a bit of an assault on the senses, and you'd need a long time behind the wheel to systematically go through any list of areas I scribble down. So, concentrate on the basics; is it tracking straight, or pulling to one side? What about under braking, or hard acceleration? You're likely to find the steering and other controls slightly heavy, unless you're used to older cars, but the S is an easy car to get to grips with.

Otherwise, it's a case of listening out for noisy transmissions or differentials, and also knocking suspension. A well-sorted S will feel quite composed, but a badly-sorted one can feel very unsettled over rough roads. Try faster gearchanges into 2nd and 3rd gear, to check for worn syncros, and when 3rd gear is selected, come on and off the power more sharply than you normally would, listening for excessive drivetrain backlash.

If you manage to find a bit of open road, accelerate hard and check that there are no flat spots up the rev range. The 2.8 V6 can feel a bit 'flat' when pushing on, as there is no sudden power-band 'kick.' The 2.9 feels very slightly livelier, though the engine snarls more aggressively due to the open air filter, while the exhaust is slightly quieter and less intrusive than the 2.8 cars. The V8S will readily administer a kick in the back, and should pull hard up to around 5500rpm. Revving it this high is pointless, day to day, but you need to make sure it doesn't become breathless at 4000-4500rpm, which could be the sign of a worn camshaft.

The best S-Series do tend to have one thing in common, however: none of them rattle. An S that feels as tightly screwed together as a modern car, even with the roof up, is a rare thing. If the doors, windows, roof and bonnet aren't squeaking, creaking, knocking or thumping, that's a very good sign! Remember to drive it with the roof on, too, otherwise the sound of a problem might be drowned out by wind and a noisy exhaust.

Onto the chassis, and some words of advice

If the chassis is covered in underseal, scrutinise the whole chassis. If you spot surface rust anywhere, scrutinise the whole chassis. If you spot some welding that clearly wasn't carried out when the car was built, scrutinise the whole chassis.

If you spot anything that doesn't look original, find a way to inspect it. This weld covered only the bottom half of the tube! (Southways Automotive Ltd)

Outriggers

A car advertised as having had 'new outriggers' isn't always a good thing. You're just as likely to find a car with bodged outriggers as you are good ones, no matter who did the work. Try and make sure the body was removed, or at least lifted, in order to carry this out. Start inspecting by lying alongside the car and locating the front corners immediately behind the wheelarch. Look for holes, flaking rust, any paint that's been applied over rust and any lumpy/ bumpy welding. The position of the body restricts your access to get in there closely, but poke any area in the corner as best you can, and assess it. Follow the tube inwards towards the rectangular lower chassis rails, and inspect the

The outriggers are the most likely area to have rusted, or show signs of previous repair. (Southways Automotive Ltd)

diagonal brace that comes down and meets the outrigger in the wheelarch. This tends to rot at the base. Now move along the length of the outrigger side tube. The front end tends to rot first, but in the event that the front end has been repaired, the centre may be about to follow. Pay particular attention to the area directly in line with the door handles too, as there is a seatbelt mounting here.

Lower rails ④ ③ ② ①

The outriggers meet the rectangular lower chassis rails at the front and centre sections. The triangular gusset plate is a common area to find corrosion or holing, especially above the plate behind the rubber mounting pads. This, along with

The rectangular lower chassis rails are paramount to the chassis' structural integrity. They tend to rust on the sides, rather than top or bottom. (Southways Automotive Ltd)

the rear inner body mounting area, are the most likely places you'll find trouble, but check all along these rails on both sides for any signs of rust or holing.

Upper rails ④ ③ ② ①

The round upper chassis rails are another area that fails to escape the clutches of corrosion. Primarily concerning the areas around the front upper wishbones, and the sections directly below the exhaust headers (where the heat generated can damage the original powdercoating), the surface can corrode heavily on this structural section.

Rear beam ④ ③ ② ①

The rear beam is twice the diameter of the outriggers, and protrudes out from the lower chassis rail near the differential, towards the end of the outrigger tube. This beam is crucial – it's the most important aspect of the chassis to check. First, get a screwdriver and (with the seller's permission) poke around the inside of the trailing arm mounts, as this area fills up with dirt and debris from the road, which retains moisture and accelerates the rusting process. The outer mounts are always worse, so if the outer ones check out, the inners are likely to be OK. Check also the angled plate at the end of the rear beam tube. The nut you can see is another of the seatbelt mountings, so it's crucial that the metal tab it's affixed to is structurally solid. Follow that tab downwards and you've found the outer body mounting (also known as the saddle mount). There will be some rubber packing between the body and the mount (completely normal), but holes tend to form underneath this mount, so you'll need your torch and

This bit's pivotal; the rear beam is probably the most important area you need to check. Make sure there are no holes, no heavy rust, and no evidence of a cover-up. (Southways Automotive Ltd)

poking device to go looking for holes. If there is a hole in any of the areas the rear beam suffers in, it's a body off repair; nothing else works. With that in mind, check very carefully for evidence of previous repairs, as some of the bodge jobs that have been seen over the years are truly horrifying when concerning a component that attaches an entire suspension arm.

Trailing arms

The round tube that runs front-to-rear on the trailing arms points downwards, with resultant rusting from the inside out, as the moisture has nowhere to escape. (Southways Automotive Ltd)

Like the rear beam, the arms themselves suffer from corrosion. The difference here is that due to the way they're designed, they tend to rust from the inside out. This is much trickier to assess than external corrosion, so the best thing you can do is gauge how they look externally and make your judgement. Anything heavily rusted on the outside stands a good chance of being weakened through internal corrosion.

Rear turrets

The rear turrets are the rectangular sections protruding upwards from the rear beam, housing the rear dampers at the highest point on the chassis. These are made of thicker gauge steel than the outriggers, and are braced in their weakest areas. They still suffer from rust, especially around the lower section, and in my experience any serious corrosion here only goes hand-in-hand with serious corrosion on the rear beam.

The rear turrets can be located here on the far right, extending up to mount the top of the damper. (Southways Automotive Ltd)

Wishbones

Obviously, wishbones are not a part of the chassis, but you may as well regard them as such if they're rusted. They're unavailable new, so buying used or repairing your old ones will be your only options. It's rare to see one holed, but bear in mind that rusty wishbones and worn bushes go hand in hand; you rarely have one without the other, and the costs mount up.

Fuel tank cradle

Another removable part like the wishbones, the cradle is home to the fuel tank, and is bolted to the rear end of the chassis. More importantly, it supports the rear weight of the body tub which, left to its own devices, would sag heavily. A result of the rear section of the body tub sagging is that the roof targa panels can lose tension, and in extreme cases they've been known to pop out of the roof aperture while on the move! The strength of the fuel tank cradle is therefore important, though these are normally available as an off-the-shelf part. They tend to rust at the extreme rear first, so check for corrosion along the lowest edge.

Both the wishbones and fuel tank cradle are bolt-on parts, but they're still important, so check carefully. These two have been refurbished, along with the chassis. (Southways Automotive Ltd)

Evaluation procedure

Add up the total points
Score: 156 excellent, 117 good, 78 average, 39 poor

Excellent cars should be close to concours standard, with only a few minor faults. Good cars should be reliable runners, with few faults; hopefully nothing that needs immediate attention, but the assessment should highlight any that do. Average cars will have a number of problems, both minor and major, and will need a careful assessment of the problems and related costs if you are prepared to fix them. Poor cars will potentially need a full restoration.

10 Auctions
– sold! Another way to buy your dream

Auction pros & cons
Pros: For the most part, prices will be lower than those of dealers or private sellers, so you might grab a real bargain on the day. Auctioneers will usually have established clear title with the seller. You can usually examine documentation relating to the vehicle at the venue.

Cons: You have to rely on a sketchy catalogue description of condition and history. The opportunity to inspect is limited and you can't drive the car. Auction cars are often a little below par and may require some work. It's easy to overbid. There will usually be a buyer's premium to pay in addition to the auction hammer price.

Which auction?
Auctions by established auctioneers are advertised in car magazines and on the auction houses' websites. A catalogue, or a simple printed list of the lots for auctions, might only be available a day or two ahead, though often lots are listed and pictured on auctioneers' websites much earlier. Contact the auction company to ask if previous auction selling prices are available, as this is useful information (details of past sales are often available on websites).

Catalogue, entry fee and payment details
When you purchase the catalogue of the vehicles in the auction, it often acts as a ticket allowing two people to attend the viewing days and the auction. Catalogue details tend to be comparatively brief, but will include information such as 'one owner from new, low mileage, full service history,' etc. It will also usually show a guide price to give you some idea of what you can expect to pay, and will tell you what is charged as a 'buyer's premium.' The catalogue will also contain details of acceptable forms of payment. At the fall of the hammer, an immediate deposit is usually required, the balance payable within 24 hours. If the plan is to pay by cash, there may be a cash limit. Some auctions will accept payment by debit card. Sometimes credit or charge cards are acceptable, but will often incur an extra charge. A bank draft or bank transfer will have to be arranged in advance with your own bank, as well as with the auction house. No car will be released before **all** payments are cleared. If delays occur in payment transfers then you may have to pay storage costs.

Buyer's premium
A buyer's premium will be added to the hammer price: **don't** forget this in your calculations. There usually won't be a further state or local tax on the purchase price and/or on the buyer's premium.

Viewing
In some instances, it's possible to view on the day, or days before, as well as in the hours prior to the auction. There are auction officials available who are willing to help out by opening engine and luggage compartments to allow you to inspect the interior. While the officials may start the engine for you, a test drive is out of the question. Crawling under and around the car as much as you want is permitted, but

you can't ask for it to be jacked up, or attempt to do the job yourself. You can also ask to see any available documentation.

Bidding

Before you take part in the auction, **decide your maximum bid – and stick to it!**

It may take a while for the auctioneer to reach the lot you are interested in, so use that time to observe how other bidders behave. When it's your car's turn, attract the auctioneer's attention and make an early bid. The auctioneer will then look to you for a reaction every time another bid is made. The bids will usually be in fixed increments until the bidding slows, whereupon smaller increments will often be accepted, before the hammer falls. If you want to withdraw from the bidding, make sure the auctioneer understands your intentions – a vigorous shake of the head when he or she looks to you for the next bid should do the trick.

Assuming you're the successful bidder, the auctioneer will note your card or paddle number, and from that moment on you will be responsible for the vehicle.

If the car is unsold, either because it failed to reach the reserve or because there was little interest, it may be possible to negotiate with the owner (via the auctioneers) after the sale is over.

Successful bid

There are two more things to think about: how to get the car home, and insurance. If you can't drive the car, you can hire a trailer (or use your own), or you can have the vehicle shipped, using a local company. The auction house will have details of companies specialising in the transfer of cars.

Insurance for immediate cover can usually be purchased on site, but it may be more cost-effective to make arrangements with your own insurance company in advance, then call to confirm the full details.

eBay & other online auctions?

eBay and other online auctions could land you a car at a bargain price, though it would be foolhardy to bid without examining the car first (something most vendors encourage). A useful feature of eBay is that the geographic location of the car is shown, so you can narrow your choices to those within a realistic distance. Be prepared to be outbid in the last few moments of the auction. Remember, your bid is binding, and it will be very difficult to get restitution if you get fleeced by a crooked vendor.

Be aware that some cars offered for sale in online auctions are 'ghost' cars. **Don't** part with **any** cash without being sure that the vehicle actually exists, and is as described (pre-bidding inspection is usually possible).

Auctioneers

Barrett-Jackson
www.barrett-jackson.com
Bonhams www.bonhams.com
British Car Auctions BCA)
www.bca-europe.com or
www.british-car-auctions co.uk
Cheffins www.cheffins.co.uk

Christies www.christies.com
Coys www.coys.co.uk
eBay www.eBay.com
H&H www.classic-auctions.co.uk
RM www.rmauctions.com
Shannons www.shannons.com.au
Silver www.silverauctions.com

11 Paperwork
– correct documentation is essential!

The paper trail
Classic, collector and prestige cars usually come with a lot of paperwork, accumulated by a succession of proud owners. This represents the real history of the car, and it can be used to deduce the level of care the car has received, how much it's been used, which specialists have worked on it and the dates of major repairs and restorations. All of this information will be priceless to you, so be very wary of cars with little paperwork to support their claimed history.

Registration documents
All countries/states have some form of registration for private vehicles, whether its the American 'pink slip' system or the British 'log book' system.

It's essential to check that the registration document is genuine, that it relates to the car, and that all the details are correctly recorded, including chassis/VIN and engine numbers (if shown). If you're buying from the previous owner, his or her name and address will be recorded; this won't be the case if you're buying from a dealer.

In the UK, the current (Euro-aligned) registration document is the 'V5C,' which has blue, green and pink sections. The blue section relates to the car specification, green has details of the new owner, and pink is sent to the DVLA in the UK, when the car is sold. A small yellow section deals with selling the car within the motor trade.

In the UK, the DVLA will provide details of earlier keepers of the vehicle, upon payment of a small fee; much can be learned in this way.

If the car has a foreign registration, there may be expensive and time-consuming formalities to complete; do you really want the hassle?

Roadworthiness certificate
Most country/state administrations require that vehicles are regularly tested to prove that they are safe to use on the public highway and do not produce excessive emissions. In the UK, that test (the 'MoT') is carried out at approved testing stations, for a fee. In the USA, most states insist on an emissions test every two years as a minimum, while the police are charged with pulling over unsafe-looking vehicles.

In the UK, the test is required on an annual basis once a vehicle reaches three years old. Of particular relevance for older cars is that the certificate issued includes the mileage reading recorded at the test date, and therefore becomes an independent record of that car's history. Ask the seller if previous certificates are available. Without an MoT, the vehicle should be trailored to its new home, unless you insist that a valid MoT is part of the deal. (This is not such a bad idea, as at least you will know the car was roadworthy on the day it was tested, and you don't need to wait for the old certificate to expire before having the test done.) In May 2018, the DVSA introduced a scheme where cars over 40 years old are offered an exemption from the MoT test (at the time of writing, the oldest S1 is 31 years old).

Road licence
The administration of every country/state charges a tax for the use of its road system. The form of the 'road licence,' and how it's displayed, varyies greatly.

Whatever the form of the 'road licence,' it must relate to the vehicle carrying it, and must be present and valid if the car is to be driven on the public highway legally. The value of the license will depend on the length of time it will continue to be valid.

In the UK, if a car is untaxed because it hasn't been used for a period of time, the owner has to inform the licencing authorities, otherwise the vehicle's date-related registration number will be lost and there will be a painful amount of paperwork to get it re-registered. Also in the UK, Classic car owners have to apply for the vehicle to be road taxed annually, but the tax is free if the car is over 40 years old on the application date.

Certificates of authenticity

For many makes of collectible car, you can get a certificate proving the vehicle's age and authenticity (eg engine and chassis numbers, paint colour and trim). These are sometimes called 'Heritage Certificates,' and if the car comes with one of these it's a definite bonus. If you want one, the relevant owners' club is the best starting point.

If the car has been used in European classic car rallies, it may have a FIVA (Federation Internationale des Vehicules Anciens) certificate. The so-called 'FIVA Passport,' or 'FIVA Vehicle Identity Card,' enables organisers and participants to recognise whether or not a particular vehicle is suitable for individual events. If you want to obtain such a certificate go to www.fbhvc.co.uk or www.fiva.org (there will be similar organisations in other countries too).

Valuation certificate

Hopefully, the vendor will have a recent valuation certificate or letter signed by a recognised expert, stating how much he or she believes the car to be worth (such documents, together with photos, are usually needed to get 'agreed value' insurance). These should act only as confirmation of your own assessment of the car, rather than a guarantee of value, as the expert probably hasn't seen the car in the flesh. The easiest way to find out how to obtain a formal valuation is to contact the owners' club.

Service history

Often, these cars will have been serviced at home by enthusiastic owners for a good number of years. Try to obtain as much service history and other paperwork as you can. Dealer stamps, or specialist garage receipts, score most points in the value stakes, but anything helps, with items like the original bill of sale, handbook, parts invoices and repair bills adding to the story and character of the car. Even a brochure correct to the year of the car's manufacture is useful, and it's something you might have to search hard to find in future years. If the seller claims the car has been restored, then expect receipts and other evidence from a specialist restorer.

If the seller claims to have carried out regular servicing, ask what work was completed when, and seek some evidence of it being carried out. Your assessment of the car's overall condition should tell you whether the seller's claims are genuine.

Restoration photographs

If the seller tells you that the car has been restored, then expect to be shown a series of photographs taken while the restoration was under way. These should help you gauge the thoroughness of the work. If you buy the car, ask if you can have all the photos, as they form an important part of the vehicle's history. A lot of sellers are happy to part with their car and accept your cash, but want to hang on to their photo! You may be able to persuade them to get a set of copies made.

12 What's it worth?
– let your head rule your heart

The chassis is the biggest influence on the value of a chosen model, simply because it's the most costly thing to put right. There are three conditions your chosen car's chassis will fall under:

Original
Aside from the rare occasion you find a car with an original, sound chassis, an unrestored chassis will likely need some work. Budget accordingly, because the cost of repairs may amount to more than the value of the car.

Repaired with body on
Body on is a method chosen purely to save time and costs. Rusted sections of the chassis will be repaired and repainted (normally the outriggers or sections visible in the wheelarches) working within the limited access possible while the body is in-situ. It's a localised repair, though (eg a new set of outriggers doesn't mean the rest of the chassis is solid). Be aware that as some cars may have been repaired poorly, they are worth no more than a project car, because they'll need the same work to put right.

Body on repairs are acceptable, if the work is good, but this outrigger repair looked fine from underneath until it was shotblasted! (Southways Automotive Ltd)

Restored with body off
Cars that have had body off chassis refurbishments are the best place to put your money, without doubt, because the chassis should have been examined closely, repaired, and then coated. Invariably, repairers have to attend to more than just the chassis, and many mechanical components are renewed at the same time. The cost to have a chassis overhauled professionally is rarely fully recovered in the future value of the car, so it's better value to buy a car that has been overhauled already. Who carried out the refurb? What chassis coating was used? (Some are much better than others!) If the refurbishment was of good quality, expect to pay around 40-60% more for a car which has been subject to a body off restoration.

A body off chassis restoration extends to much more than just the chassis. (Southways Automotive Ltd)

The paintwork and interior are a much more subjective topic. What one person considers show-worthy, another may consider atrocious! The only advice I can give you here is to set your expectations and stick to them. Only you know what you're happy with, or what you're willing to spend further funds on. Get some rough quotes to complete any work you're not happy with, and factor this into your negotiation.

Modifications

Many owners often add their own little touches and 'upgrades.' These play less of an impact on the residuals than with many other marques, and buyers should not be put off by a few modifications of a certain car. Many may indeed improve the car, such as retrofitting better mirrors onto an S1, or a modification to increase the opening angle of the bonnet.

Some desirable modifications to an S might include:
- Wide-opening bonnet (all models)
- Retrofitting different mirrors (early models)
- Larger front brake conversion (all models)
- Rear disc brake conversion (S1/S2/S3)
- Polyurethane suspension bushes (all models)

If a modification is reversible, then it shouldn't negatively affect the value of the car, and may well increase it if deemed desirable by the majority. If it's effectively an irreversible modification, such as an engine conversion, then it is simply down to the buyer's own tastes as to how the value is affected. Generally speaking, body modifications will have a negative impact on the value of a car, as will the removal of hard-to-find parts, such as original wheels or interiors, because a heavily modified S has a narrower potential market than an original car. For somebody who wants a car of that exact spec, however, it might be worth more!

Access to this V8S's engine bay has dramatically improved. (S Tyree)

This S3 has changed a bit since it left Bristol Avenue; that's a Jaguar V6 engine! (D Ward)

Paperwork & provenance

Mechanically, the S-Series is a tough car. The components used on it were designed to propel much larger, heavier cars up and down motorways; day in, day out. They're largely under-stressed, and for the most part, reliable. A sign of a looked-after car is a privately-advertised car being sold by a member of a TVR Car Club (especially if they're replacing the S with another model of the same marque) as nobody would knowingly sell a poor car when there's a chance you'll meet each other again at the next gathering! Service history also plays a part in a classic car's value, as the story of how the car arrived at where it is today is a strong selling tool. Evidence that the car has been mechanically cared for over the years is always desirable, and if somebody agonised looking after the paperwork and written history of the car, the odds are they took the time to look after the car itself too.

Valuations

For UK-based cars, the TVR Car Club are able to provide members with realistic valuations based on current market trends, which also take into account rarity, originality and provenance. TVRs also feature regularly in the motoring press, including classic car magazines who have run buying guides and features on the model in recent years.

13 Do you really want to restore?

– it'll take longer and cost more than you think

You need to ask yourself a key question in order to decide whether or not it's financially viable to buy an S and restore it: Can *you* do the work (or at least the bulk of it) yourself? If you can, then there's a good chance you'll end up with a cracking car, which also happens to be good value for money.

However, if you can't, you need to ask yourself another question: How concerned are you about seeing a return on your investment? Sounds silly, but some owners are happy to pay for their dream car to be built to the highest standard it can be, regardless of cost. That's great, if money is no object. But if money *is* an object (as it is for most people) then you should think carefully about your options.

The biggest issue with restoring an S is that it'll almost certainly cost more than the market value of the car to complete to a good standard. Even with a V8S, a full respray, chassis restoration, and interior re-trim will easily surpass the value of the car, should you decide to move it on. Granted, they're climbing in value, but how quickly?

People who tend to have their cars overhauled by a professional outfit are normally long-time owners of a car already. They've developed an emotional commitment to it, far above any monetary value. Should these end up on the market, they're unquestionably the

"Erm ... now what?!"
(M Lacroix)

best cars to buy, because they will have been maintained to a high standard, regardless of expense.

In the event you decide to buy a project S, and restore it yourself (or at least carry out the majority of the labour), you could still quite easily spend the average market value of that model in parts or specialist services alone. However, at the end of it you will at least have a car in far better order than the average market-priced example, and possibly make good on your investment.

In terms of the skill level needed to tackle an S, there's nothing particularly challenging to concern yourself with. Time-consuming they may be, and there are certainly areas where experience helps (like

This V8S is the fourth example built by TVR. It's going to take more than its market value to get it back to its former glory, though. (G Haydon/ Southways Automotive Ltd)

aligning bonnets), but from a DIY point of view, they should prove an enjoyable restoration. And if you're someone who enjoys tinkering and trying to improve the way things work, you'll find plenty to play with in an S!

14 Paint problems
– bad complexion, including dimples, pimples and bubbles

Paint faults generally occur due to lack of protection/maintenance, or to poor preparation prior to a respray or touch-up. Some of the following conditions may be present in the car you're looking at:

Orange peel

This appears as an uneven paint surface, similar to the appearance of the skin of an orange. The fault is caused by the failure of atomized paint droplets to flow into each other when they hit the surface. It's sometimes possible to rub out the effect with proprietory paint cutting/rubbing compound, or very fine grades of abrasive paper. A respray may be necessary in severe cases. Consult a bodywork repairer/paint shop for advice on the particular car.

Orange peel.

Cracking

Severe cases are likely to have been caused by too heavy an application of paint (or filler beneath the paint). Also, insufficient stirring of the paint before application can lead to the components being improperly mixed, and cracking can result. Incompatibility with the paint already on the panel can have a similar effect. To rectify the problem, it's necessary to rub down to a smooth, sound finish before respraying the problem area.

With a GRP body comes specific GRP problems, like this crack in the gel coat.

Crazing

Sometimes the paint takes on a crazed rather than cracked appearance, when the problems mentioned under 'Cracking' are present. This problem can also be caused by a reaction between the underlying surface and the paint. Removing the paint and respraying the problem area is usually the only solution.

Cracking and crazing.

Blistering

Almost always caused by corrosion of the metal beneath the paint. Usually, perforation will be found in the metal and the damage will be worse than that suggested by the area of blistering. The metal will have to be repaired before repainting.

Micro blistering
Usually the result of an economy respray, where inadequate heating has allowed moisture to settle on the car before spraying. Consult a paint specialist, but usually damaged paint will have to be removed before partial or full respraying. Can also be caused by car covers that don't 'breathe.'

Blistering.

Fading
Some colours, especially reds, are prone to fading if subjected to strong sunlight for long periods, without the benefit of polish protection. Sometimes proprietary paint restorers, and/or paint cutting/ rubbing compounds, will retrieve the situation. Often a respray is the only real solution.

Micro blistering.

Peeling
Often a problem with metallic paintwork, when the sealing laquer becomes damaged and begins to peel off. Poorly applied paint may also peel. The remedy is to strip and start again!

Dimples
Dimples in the paintwork are caused by the residue of polish (particularly silicone types) not being removed properly before respraying. Paint removal and repainting is the only solution.

Dents
Small dents are usually easily cured by the 'Dentmaster,' or equivalent process, that sucks or pushes out the dent (as long as the paint surface is still intact). Companies offering dent removal services usually come to your home – consult your telephone directory.

15 Problems due to lack of use
– just like their owners, S-Series need exercise!

The S dislikes sitting around doing nothing as much as any other car, and while some vehicles will have lived a life of luxury in a dehumidified garage, many won't. While the usual checks for any classic or specialist vehicle will apply, there are some areas on an S that you need to pay attention to:

Not all S-Series have lived their lives in a garage as nice as this!

Roof & rear screen
This needs to be flexible on an S, as it's contorted and compressed when the roof is collapsed. Long periods of exposure to sunlight will harden a rear screen, and it will probably fracture after a few attempts. The fabric can also lose adhesion to the roof framework and, in some cases, shrink to the point that a retrim is required.

Rubber components
These are particularly susceptible to periods of disuse. This could include coolant hoses, vacuum hoses, fuel hoses and all suspension bushes and rubber body mountings on the car. The fuel lines in particular are worth checking closely, because all S-Series are fuel-injected, and therefore any leaks on the supply side will be under pressure. Along with the coolant hoses, inspect the radiator closely for any signs of leaks or heavy corrosion.

Front brake calipers
Front brake calipers on an S (along with the rears on a V8S or S4C) are all of the floating variety. This means that along with potentially seized pistons, you also run the risk of seized slider pins. A single caliper won't break the bank, but if all four need sorting, the costs could escalate quickly.

Bonnet release mechanisms
These can be a potential headache because if the cable(s) snap, entry to the engine bay will prove extremely difficult. Check that the lever moves freely, and that the cable and locks show no signs of sticking, as repair/replacement is difficult.

Corroded electrical contacts

This can cause all manner of problems, especially on the 2.9 V6 models. Many of the connectors across the range also use a rubber seal to keep them safe from damp, and if these are missing (as they frequently are) damp could form inside, causing corrosion which can heat up due to resistance and melt the connector body itself.

Rusted fuel tanks & exhausts

This can cause trouble later on. Any rust inside either may not present a problem until a number of miles have passed under the wheels. In the case of the fuel tank, there's a small pre-filter in the 'sump' of the tank, which can become blocked over and over again when trying to press a once-dormant vehicle back into regular service.

A car that has been standing is a risk, but it could be worth taking if you enjoy the repair work.

Interior materials

These tended to vary in their quality from the factory, and some cars will have deteriorated worse than others. Don't dismiss a tired interior – the cost to put one right could equate to the difference between the car you bought, and another one you wanted more, but thought you couldn't afford.

Sticky clutch

Any evidence of a sticky clutch shouldn't be ignored. While you might be tempted to pass it off as something that 'just needs freeing off,' the reality is that the clutch will probably need changing and, as mentioned previously, it's an engine-out job. The flywheel will likely need refacing too, so though it's not a reason to walk away, consider the added costs and hassle involved. Also consider that, though the clutch hydraulics may be functioning happily now, perished or tired rubber will likely lead to a failed seal later down the line, though at least these are more simple fixes.

Tyres

Pay close attention to the tyres. Periods of long-standing can lead to flat spots and misshapen rubber, which in turn can lead to vibrations, reduced grip and, in extreme cases, tyre failure. Check the rubber is not hard and that the sidewalls are free from cracking.

Chassis

This can rust, even in a garage! All the previous mentions of chassis condition apply to all cars, including the ones that sit indoors not doing anything.

16 The Community

– key people, organisations and companies in the S-Series world

Clubs

UK
TVR Car Club – 01952 822126
– tvr-car-club.co.uk
Belgium
tvrcarclub.be
France
tvrcarclub-france.net
Germany
tvrcarclub.de

Italy
tvrcarclubitalia.com
Japan
tvrccj.net
Netherlands
tvrcarclub.nl
North America (inc Canada)
tvrccna.org
Sweden
tvrcc.se

Bodywork

- Classic Restore (Hampshire) – 023 8061 3612 – www.classicrestore.co.uk
- Option 1 (Worcestershire) – 01527 557111 – www.option1sportscars.co.uk
- Surface & Design Ltd (Lancashire) – 01253 595800 – wwwsurfaceanddesign.com

Chassis

- Mat Smith Sports Cars (Norfolk) – 01366 386004 – matsmithsportscars.com
  RT Racing (S. Yorkshire) – 0114 281 7507 – rtracing.co.uk
- Southways Automotive (Hampshire) – 01329 220755
  – southwaysautomotive.co.uk
- Sportmotive (Staffordshire) – 01782 333008 – sportmotive.com
- Str8six (Oxfordshire) – 01844 352735 – str8six.co.uk

Interior

- Dave The Trimmer (Bedfordshire) – 01908 585 039
  – davethetrimmer.com/index.html
- D&C Trim (Lancashire) – 07738 130236 – dctrim.co.uk/home.html
- Trim Unique (Lancashire) – 07885 990113 – trim-unique.co.uk

Mechanical

- Classic World Racing (Worcestershire) – 01527 521050
  – classicworldracing.webmate.me
- Lawfield Engineering (Lancashire) – 07810 018747
- Powers Performance (W. Midlands) – 024 7636 6177 – powersperformance.co.uk
- SD Autotec (N. Yorkshire) – 01423 329090 – sdautotec.co.uk
- Southways Automotive (Hampshire) – 01329 220755 – southwaysautomotive.co.uk
- TVRSSW (Somerset) – 01823 662555 – tvrssw.com
- X-Works (Lancashire) – 01772 937177 – xworksservice.co.uk

Parts

- ACT Performance Products – 01342 311790 – actproducts.co.uk
- Racetech Direct – 01491 629219 – racetechdirect.co.uk
- RT Racing – 0114 281 7507 – rtracing.co.uk
- TVR Parts Ltd (TVR's official parts network) – 03333 237877 – tvr-parts.com

Ownership community & social scene:
- Facebook – facebook.com/groups/tvrsseries
- Pistonheads – pistonheads.com/gassing (go to TVR subforum – select S Series)
- TVRCC UK S-Series info – tvr-car-club.co.uk/tvr-s-series.html
- Fast Track Tours – fasttracktours.co.uk

**'S Club Heaven' events are an annual meet specifically for the S-Series,
whilst owners regularly enjoy epic touring holidays provided by
the likes of Fast Track Tours.**

Annual gatherings (known as 'S-Club Heaven') meet at different locations around the UK each year, and companies such as Fast Track Tours (created by a long-time S owner) offer the chance to partake in fantastic driving holidays both around the UK and in Europe, created specifically for you to enjoy the best an S has to offer.

One of the best aspects of the S-Series, as a model, is the community of owners that surround it. You're unlikely to find a more approachable, friendly, and down to Earth collective in many one-make ownership circles, and one of the plus points for owning an S is being a part of that. Each chapter in this book features a header image of a current owner's car to reflect the 'community spirit' the car captures, and I'd like to thank everybody who submitted an image for me to use.

- Wheelbase: 2286mm (90in)
- Length: 3957mm (155.8in)
- Width: 1666mm (65.6in)
- Height: 1220mm (48in)
- Fuel tank capacity: 55L (12UK Gal)
- Steering: rack & pinion (manual)
- Wheel size: 7Jx15
- Tyre: 205/60R15 (V-rated)

S1

- Production: 1986-1989
- Engine: Ford – 2792cc OHV V6
- Max power (claimed): 160bhp (119kW) @ 5700rpm
- Peak torque: 163lbft (220Nm) @ 4300rpm
- Top speed: 128mph (207km/h)
- 0-60mph: 7.6secs
- Kerb weight: 950kg (approx.)
- Fuel system: Bosch K-Jetronic fuel-injection
- Brakes F/R: (V)Disc/Drum
- Differential type: open
- Door version: short
- Factory chassis colour(s): white; black

S2/S3/S3C/S4C

- Production: 1988-1994
- Engine: Ford – 2933cc OHV V6
- Max power (claimed): 168bhp (125kW) @ 6000rpm ('C' model suffers marginal loss)
- Peak torque: 172bft (233Nm) @ 3000rpm ('C' model suffers marginal loss)
- Top speed: 130mph (209km/h)
- 0-60mph: 6.9secs
- Kerb weight: 980kg (approx.)
- Fuel system: Ford EEC Electronic fuel-injection
- Brakes F/R: (V)Disc/Drum (S4C: Disc/Disc)
- Differential type: open (S4C: Viscous limited-slip)
- Door version: short (S2) Long (S3/S4)
- Factory chassis colour(s): white; black; dark red

Max Unwin's V8S looking resplendent wearing Estoril alloy wheels from a Griffith 500. (K Dunnington)

Craig Brown's S4C made it all the way from Blackpool to New Zealand! (C Brown)

The driver of this S3 enjoying Cadwell Park. (A Waddington)

V8S

- Production: 1991-1994
- Engine: Rover – 3947cc OHV V8
- Max power (claimed): 240bhp (179kW) @ 5250rpm
- Peak torque: 270lbft (366Nm) @ 3000rpm
- Top speed: 147mph (209km/h)
- 0-60mph: 5.2secs
- Kerb weight: 1050kg
- Fuel system: Lucas electronic fuel-injection
- Brakes F/R: (V)Disc/Disc
- Differential type: viscous limited-slip
- Door version: long
- Factory chassis colour(s): dark red

S-Series on tour in Scotland, 2017. (M Roberts)

Also from Veloce:

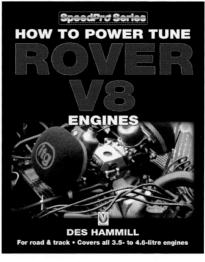

ISBN: 978-1-845842-07-9
Paperback • 25x20.7cm • 128 pages

Available again after several
months absence!

How to get the best handling and
braking from sportscars/kitcars with
wishbone front suspension, coil springs
and telescopic shock absorbers.
Includes ride height, camber, castor,
kpi and much more.

ISBN: 978-1-787111-76-9
Paperback • 25x20.7cm • 216 pages

Covers all Rover 3.5, 3.9, 4.0 & 4.6
litre engines from 1967 to date. Get
maximum road or track performance &
reliability for minimum money. The author
is an engineer with much professional
experience of building race engines.
Suitable for the enthusiast as well
as the more experienced mechanic.
All information is based on practical
experience.

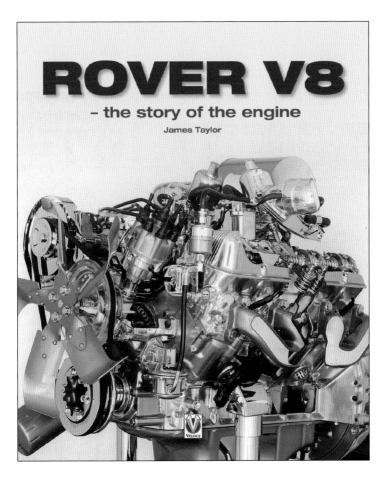

ROVER V8

– the story of the engine

James Taylor

ISBN: 978-1-787110-26-7
Hardback • 25x20.7cm • 144 pages • 170 colour and b&w pictures

This book tells the full story of the Rover V8 engine, its origins as a General Motors design in the 1950s and its development by Rover (and subsequently Land Rover) between 1967 and 2004. It focuses on production versions of the engine and includes information supplied by those who worked on its design and development.

The Essential Buyer's Guide™ series ...